How to Connect with Your Audience & Build a 5-Star Brand Reputation

Allison McIntyre Cain

Copyright © 2018 Allison McIntyre Cain

All rights reserved.

All rights reserved regarding in this book. No part of any of these may be reproduced or transmitted in any form or by any means, electronic or mechanical, including photocopying, recording, or by any information storage and retrieval system, without written permission from the publisher, except for brief quotations used in critical reviews and other noncommercial uses permitted by copyright law. For permission requests, contact:

McCain and Associates, LLC Publishing
20 Ferguson Circle
Midway, GA 31320
Phone: (912) 463-3323
Web: http://mccainandassociates.com
Email: mcaallc@gmail.com

Ordering Information
Individual Sales: McCain and Associates, LLC Publishing products are available through most bookstores. They can also be ordered directly from McCain and Associates, LLC at the address above.

Quantity Sales: McCain and Associates, LLC Publish products are available at special quantity discounts when purchased in bulk by corporations, churches, associations, nonprofits, libraries, and others, or for college textbook/course adoptions. Please write to the address above or call McCain and Associates, LLC Publishing Book Sales Division at 912-463-3323

ISBN-13: 978-1539109723

ISBN-10:1539109720

WORDS FROM THE WISE...

"If I take care of my character, my reputation will take care of itself."
— **D.L. Moody**

"Regard your good name as the richest jewel you can possibly be possessed of -- for credit is like fire; when once you have kindled it you may easily preserve it, but if you once extinguish it, you will find it an arduous task to rekindle it again. The way to a good reputation is to endeavor to be what you desire to appear."
— **Socrates**

"We live in a reputation economy. People are judged based on their online visible choices, behaviors, accomplishments and mistakes. Every comment you leave, person you connect to, photo you upload, or review you get, contributes to the permanent record of your online reputation."
— **Maarten Schäfer**, **Around The World in 80 Brands**

DEDICATION

I want to dedicate this book to **David Sprague** and his **Real Strategic Inc.** team for all the exceptional work you guys do. You are a great mentor, and I appreciate all that you do to make sure that we understand the importance of helping business owners have success. Taking your mastermind was and is the greatest investment I could make for myself and my business.

My goal as an Entrepreneur is to better master one of the core values I learned from you: ***Always lead with value.*** I pray this book will do just that. Thank you for being a selfless leader who creates and empowers other leaders. I will pay what you have taught me forward. ♥

If any of you readers are interested in learning more about reputation marketing, branding, visibility, and the basic of owning a business, I encourage you to look up **Local Marketing Genius Mastermind**. David Sprague will over-deliver and teach you what you need to build a 6-figure or 7-figure business. Trust him, and do exactly what he says, and you will help a lot of business owners and have lots of success.

TABLE OF CONTENTS

WORDS FROM THE WISE...   iii

DEDICATION   iv

ACKNOWLEDGMENTS   ix

INTRODUCTION   x

CHAPTER 1| CAN CONSUMERS FIND YOUR BUSINESS WHERE THEY ARE LOOKING?   - 1 -

NOTES   - 19 -

CHAPTER 2: WHAT WILL YOU SAY WHEN YOU FIND THEM?   - 20 -

NOTES   - 30 -

CHAPTER 3| DO YOU EVEN KNOW WHO THEY ARE?   - 31 -

NOTES   - 37 -

CHAPTER 4| WHAT DO THEY WANT, AND WHAT DO THEY THINK?   - 38 -

NOTES   - 43 -

CHAPTER 5| YOU GOTTA KEEP THEM INTERESTED   - 44 -

NOTES	- 48 -
CHAPTER 6 | GIVE THEM WHAT THEY WANT	- 49 -
NOTES	- 54 -
CHAPTER 7 | DO YOU KNOW WHAT OTHERS ARE SAYING ABOUT YOU?	- 55 -
NOTES	- 60 -
CHAPTER 8 | JUST SAY PLEASE	- 61 -
NOTES	- 64 -
CHAPTER 9 | WHO DID WHAT? WHEN? WHY?	- 65 -
NOTES	- 71 -
CHAPTER 10 | ALWAYS SAY THANK YOU	- 72 -
NOTES	- 76 -
CHAPTER 11 | CREATE A CULTURE OF EXCELLENCE	- 77 -
NOTES	- 82 -
CHAPTER 12 | LET THEM KNOW HOW GREAT YOU ARE	- 83 -
NOTES	- 88 -
CHAPTER 13 | ARE YOU REACHING THE RIGHT	

PEOPLE?	- 89 -
NOTES	- 93 -
CHAPTER 14 | FUNNEL MAGIC	- 94 -
NOTES	- 97 -
SUMMARY	- 98 -
ABOUT THE AUTHOR	- 99 -

ACKNOWLEDGMENTS

There is no such thing as a product or service created by just one person. Often behind the scenes, friends and family are the ones who contribute so much to our finished works. Such is the case for me completing this book.

My family continually inspires and encourages me to go after my dreams and let nothing stand in my way. I am so thankful to God for providing me with an excellent family. Beverly McIntyre, Melissa McIntyre Brandly, Anthony McIntyre, Wallace McIntyre, Adam Grant, Andrew McIntyre, Alanna McIntyre, Alan Cain, Sarah Grant, Anthony McIntyre and Annette Ferguson you all are ROCKSTARS to me, and I'm so blessed to have you in my life. Lastly but definitely not least Brian Cain, you are an important part of my life, and I'm thankful for you encouraging me to write! Thank you all for supporting me. Your love is a powerful motivator, encourager, enforcer, and keeper!

My awesome friends are always around to listen to my ideas, to give me feedback, and to support my various endeavors. I love you so much for your selflessness. Leetta Simmons, Shawn Johnson, and Desiree Lee, you ladies are thebomb.com! Thank you for being anchors in my life.

INTRODUCTION

Knowing how to connect with your customers and with potential customers is as valuable today as learning how to automate work processes was at the beginning of the Industrial Revolution. Technology continues to change how professionals do business and how consumers behave. Where once they would have depended on visiting a business and determining if they liked it after spending their money on it; today's consumer searches for online reviews about the business on their mobile devices before they ever visit the location.

The one thing that has not changed throughout the years is word of mouth is still one of the best forms of communication, and today's shoppers are going to share their experiences in your business. Instead of just telling their family and friends about their experience, today's consumer is likely going on some social media platform like Facebook, Twitter, Instagram, Snapchat, Yelp, TripAdvisor, YouTube, or Google to tell everyone they can reach. Knowing this, prepare yourself to use this information, and build a 5-Star reputation.

This is not just for businesses in the sense of brick and mortar businesses. It is for anyone who offers a product or service to consumers with the expectation that they will make sales. So, if you are a business coach, life coach, author, blogger, internet marketer, e-commerce store owner or anyone else, this book is for you!

I am going to share some valuable tips that will help you impress your prospects and better connect with them so that you are always giving them what they want in the way they want it. I have included a Notes section after each chapter for you to use. Write down things you need to do to start achieving your goals. Take Massive Imperfect Actions daily. If you follow my suggestions, you will be rewarded with more loyal customers and with a 5-Star business reputation that you can market to get more customers. Are you ready? Then let's get started. ♥A.M.C. ♥

CHAPTER 1 | CAN CONSUMERS FIND YOUR BUSINESS WHERE THEY ARE LOOKING?

The title of this chapter may seem silly to the average person, but you are NOT average. You are wise and perceptive enough to realize that your target customers may not be searching for businesses like yours in the same places that they used to look for them.

Once upon a time, the Yellow Pages, radio, television, and newspapers were ideal for reaching your customers and prospective customers. Today, those mediums are not as effective for connecting. If you want to reach your target audience today, you are going to have to invest in learning social media platforms and in customizing your business information in the way those platforms require.

This century has been and will be grounded in relationship marketing. Developing healthy relationships with your customers and the communities you've built on social media platforms are critical for your business to grow to its next level. Those who put in the time, money, and effort will reap a continual harvest of customers. Those who refuse to make the investments will be run over and run out of business by their greatest rival: **CHANGE**.

I know that change is scary to some, but it does not have to be. When you're armed with knowledge and courage, you can navigate the turbulent waters of technology and change that are introduced into the marketplace daily.

What you should be afraid of is doing nothing. I think it was Einstein who said that doing the same thing over and over but expecting a different result was the very definition of Insanity. Since we have already established that you are wise and perceptive, we only need to get you the right information to courageously take massive imperfect actions.

I know what you're probably thinking—you do Not take imperfect actions because people will talk trash about you, but I promise that is not so if you play your cards right; and you guessed it—I'm going to show you how to play the hand you have to win.

So, let's dive in and learn where your target audience is hanging so that you can reach out and connect with them to offer great deals, top-quality products/services, and win their loyalty. 😊

There are too many social media platforms for me to talk about all of them, so I am going to encourage you to have a professional business page on the following social media platforms: Facebook, Twitter, Snapchat, Instagram, Google+, YouTube, Pinterest, and LinkedIn. Each of these platforms appeals to different demographics of people for different reasons; so, you decide which individually or collectively will resonate with your customers and target customers.

I am going to spend a little time on Facebook because it has the largest number of subscribers and can provide unlimited leads when used effectively. This does not mean you should only focus on this platform. Take the information I give you for Facebook and apply it to all the platforms that your target audience uses.

Facebook: At the time of this writing, Facebook has over 2 billion subscribers. That is too many people to ignore. In fact, it is too many people that you can target to generate more consistent and predictable revenue streams. If you do any research on this platform, you will be amazed at the amount of time the average subscriber spends here and the level of information they share about themselves.

Because there are various aspects to completing a profile, Facebook is one of the best places to share information about your business with consumers who have said they like services/products like the ones you sell. Moreover, to make this platform even more enticing, CEO Mark Zuckerberg and his team continue to add features that engage its subscribers for longer amounts of time.

According to Facebook, as of July 27, 2016 more than 1.13 billion of its customers are active and log in daily. 76% are female while 66% are male, and more than 16 million businesses have created fan pages. What does this mean to you? The answer may shock you. Having your business adequately represented on Facebook can increase your visibility more than most of the traditional ways that used to be so effective.

What do I mean when I say, "adequately represented"? I mean that you should have a fan page that has been optimized to reach your target audience. Search Engine Optimization (SEO) is important part of your business coming up when consumers are searching for a business. That is a fancy way of saying it should be enhanced or improved to include the various keywords that your prospects will use when searching for businesses like yours.

For example, if you have an HVAC company in Charlotte, North Carolina you want to make sure that in addition to your name on your fan page you include the city and state. You can create a title that includes some the terms a person searching for an HVAC specialist would cover like emergency HVAC services or HVAC repair.

If you do not know what terms a person is using, then I suggest you learn how to use a keyword tool like Google has. It will give you the specific words that people use to search online for what they want. It will also give you ideas if you do not know where to start. Let's take a look at an example of Google's Keyword Tool in action using the example of the Charlotte, NC HVAC.

Keyword (by relevance)	Avg. monthly searches	Competition	Suggested bid
hvac charlotte nc	100 – 1K	High	$51.42
heating and air charlotte nc	100 – 1K	High	$48.38
hvac repair charlotte nc	100 – 1K	High	$86.00
heating repair charlotte nc	100 – 1K	High	$51.99
charlotte hvac repair	10 – 100	High	–

The image shows that there between 100 and 1000

people searching for an HVAC business in Charlotte, NC. It also reveals that there are individuals who type in the following terms when they are searching for this kind of business:

Keywords:

NC

HVAC charlotte

Charlotte HVAC jobs

HVAC Charlotte NC

heating and air Charlotte NC

HVAC repair Charlotte NC

heating repair Charlotte NC

charlotte HVAC repair

emergency air conditioning repairs Charlotte NC

charlotte HVAC

charlotte heating and air

charlotte air conditioning

nc pl

heating and cooling Charlotte NC

heating repair Charlotte

air conditioning charlotte

air conditioning Charlotte NC

air conditioning repair Charlotte North Carolina

HVAC contractor Charlotte NC

platform NC

heating and air conditioning Charlotte NC

furnace repair Charlotte

HVAC service Charlotte NC

heating and air Charlotte

charlotte heating repair

From the partial (the complete list has over 700 search ideas) list above you can get a sense of what your business' fan page should include in its name, profile images, posts, and responses to comments. This will make sure that your company's Facebook page is found at the top of the list as people look for businesses like this. ♦♥

It is also important that you claim your business fan page on Facebook. Set up your Fan Page to include your hours of operation, days open, your address, your phone number, and your address. Include enticing and loveable pictures that your fans will share with their family and friends.

Check-Ins: This is such a cool feature that every business owner should use it daily. Encourage your customers to "check-in" on their mobile device when they're at your business and share pictures of them interacting with your employees. Give discounts to those who check-in and leave a review on Facebook. This is a great way for them to let their family and friends know that you're having a sale, cooked a great meal, has a special going or whatever is happening. Check-Ins are a great tool for contests, where the person with the most check-ins gets something for free. It's a win-win situation.

Cover Videos: Videos are what's happening in 2018 and beyond. It's the medium that most consumers want and use for communications. Armed with this information, Facebook allows business owners to create a cover video to use for their business' Fan Page profile image. Instead of a static image, you now can create a video from 20-90 seconds long that is at least 820x312 pixels, while the recommended size is 820x462 pixels. This is an excellent way to highlight your great discounts or sales items, 5-Star Testimonials, Before & After proofs of your workmanship, and more.

Ordering for Restaurants: Once again, Facebook has raised the bar a lot higher for other platforms to reach. If you own a restaurant, Facebook permits you to upload your menu on your business' Fan Page, and your customers can order directly from that page! This is huge because most people use Facebook on mobile devices and have the Facebook app open for long periods. Have you taken advantage of your Facebook digital storefront? If you haven't then you're missing out on customers who are looking for the easy way to order food. Don't worry if you don't know how to set this up. I can help you.

The Marketplace: What if I told you that Facebook didn't just make things good for restaurant owners—they made it wonderful for real estate agents with homes to list, car dealerships with vehicles to sell, apartment complexes with vacancies to fill, and for individuals with things to sell. That's right—Facebook has a Marketplace that will allow you to reach your target audience to sell things. Take great pictures, write interesting copy that appeals to them, and let Facebook's Audience tool help you find buyers and renters.

Retargeting: Retargeting is another tool that your company should be using to be where your customers are. Facebook, Google, and many other platforms have retargeting tools that you can use to increase your chances of getting a prospect to buy from you. So, what is retargeting? In its simplest form, retargeting is the process of creating a pixel or code that you can attach to your marketing products that will follow your prospects around on the Internet. When a prospect searches online, views your content, adds an item to a shopping cart, adds products to wish lists, adds payment information, initiates checkouts, makes purchases, completes registrations, signs up for trials, lands on a Thank You page, or opens your email but ***does NOT buy from you***, your code will follow them around the Internet and show them your business' ad, so they never forget you. Isn't that amazing?

If I were a betting woman, I'd bet money that you have already experienced re-targeting personally. Have you gone to a website to compare prices of an item like a smartphone, but you didn't purchase it? When you went to your Facebook page or some other page you found that there were ads of the very same smartphone you recently viewed. You then saw that ad in most places that you visited online. That is retargeting at its best.

Just think about this. Thomas Scott, a British merchant, noted in his book, *Successful Advertising*, that consumers needed to view a brand's ad at least 20 times before responding accordingly. This means if you are currently reaching out to your prospects one or two times before quitting, then you are leaving much money on the table.

Retargeting allows your ad to follow a prospect wherever they go online; so if someone got an email from you sharing information about a new product that intrigued them enough to visit your website, but your website didn't convert them into a paying customer a retargeting pixel would allow them to see your brand's ad when they went online to Facebook and again when they visited CNN or Fox News and again when they went on Instagram, and you get the picture.

Retargeting allows you to get your ad in front of your target audience enough times so that they feel like they know you and trust you enough to do business with you. So, don't ignore this powerful tool because it could increase your bottom line significantly. Remember what I said earlier, *"Your business will grow to the next level as you learn, adopt, and execute relationship marketing tools, tactics, and strategies."* If you are married, you probably didn't propose to your spouse after the first date. Consumers are like that too. They want to know you better before giving you their money.

If you need help setting up a retargeting campaign, my team and I will be happy to help you. Just go to http://mccainandassociates.com, and fill out the information for a FREE consultation. It is not hard to increase your visibility so that you can reach the most targeted people who want what your company provides.

Advertising on Social Media: Advertising on social media sites like Facebook, LinkedIn, Twitter, Instagram, Google, and others is one of the fastest ways that you can get your brand in front of consumers who are looking for what you have to offer.

There used to be a time when advertising seemed clumsy and a bit interfering, but not today. Most of the platforms I listed above, and many others have created ways to provide organic ads that look just like the regular posts on their sites. These ads look just like a regular post that you or your friends would post, so many people will click on them. This is so effective because if you can create an appealing image with the right message, you are going to reach far more targeted prospects.

Advertising on social media sites and other advertising platforms lets you be unique to those whom you want to see your ads and to respond. You get to customize an audience based on interests, demographic information, likes, income, even people who like your competitors. How great is that?

Traditional methods of advertising like newspapers and TV offer some of the same customizations but for a larger price and often with fewer pools of consumers. Don't forget that I said that at the time of this writing, Facebook has over 2 billion subscribers who have share very specific likes and interests. Gone are the days of throwing your advertising dollars up in the air and hoping they land on the right buyers. Social media advertising lets you find shoppers who like Prince, and who make at least $50,000 annually, who read The Wall Street Journal, who live within 50 miles of Savannah, Georgia, and who like Barack Obama and Tiger Woods. You can create an audience that will likely buy your product/service because they like other products like the ones you sell. The Newspaper and Radio can never provide this specific information when selling ads.

Another point to remember is that you should engage your target audience regularly on the social media platforms that you find are where they spend their time. This should include posts with engaging and appealing images as well as videos because that is what more and more people like.

Giving your current customers and prospects a way to

connect with you on social media platforms will help form loyalty and will allow you to educate them on your business and the products and services you offer. This is also a useful tool to know what people are saying about your brand and a way for you to respond to their comments. It is a very effective way to build and nurture relationships in the Internet Age.

I won't beat a dead horse, but it is very important for you to treat your customers and community of followers the way you would a spouse. Talk to them frequently. Find out what interests them. If they have a complaint about your business, address it honestly and promptly. Apologize even if you don't think you did anything. I don't mean a bullcrap apology. They will see through that quickly. Apologize that they experienced a negative situation to them.

I've found that asking questions like, "What can I do to make this better for you?" or "Is there anything I can do to make this better for you?" often open the door to healing and can result in a stronger relational bond. Don't talk. Let them share while you listen attentively. People often just want you to acknowledge them, so don't overlook this powerful tool.

When you create your ads to display on social media sites, it's nice to use bold colors that have high contrast. If you are using videos, don't let them Auto-play or they may be rejected. Use the tools that each platform provides. Find Third-Party data that is accurate. Use images that will attract attention like pictures of animals, people doing things, beautiful locations, and pictures that are interesting. Also, you want to make sure that your ads are compliant with the platforms' terms of service or they will reject them.

Social Directories, Review Sites & Citations: Social directories and citations are just as important as social media sites because many consumers go to them when they want to find the best product or service. The most known are Google, Bing, Yahoo, Yelp, Four Square, Insider Pages, Merchant Circle, Super Pages, Yellow Pages, Local.com, Angie's List, Kudzu, Trip Advisor, Judy's Book and a host of others. These sites are crucial because they are the place that consumers choose to find what they want, so it is imperative that your company has a profile on as many of these sites as possible. That way, you are increasing the odds that regardless of where a search is conducted, your business will be found. ♦♥

As important as being found is, having the correct information on those sites is equally as important. Why? Because if a consumer gets your company information after performing a search, the information should be accurate so that when they dial, they get your office.

I know this sounds unusually simple, but you would be amazed at the number of businesses that have out of date information listed on directory sites. If they do not have outdated information, they may have different information on them.

For example, the business phone on Yelp may be correct with 912-555-8888, but Google and Trip Advisor may have 912-555-8877. Your company would get all the calls from consumers who searched on Yelp, but it would miss all of those who used Google and Trip Advisor. How many more customers would it take to make a difference to your bottom line? What would it do to your life and your family's life if you could get three- five more daily customers who got the right telephone number on all directory sites?

In a real-life example, this could mean ten people ready to buy got the correct phone number and called you; whereas the 14 who searched on Google and the eight who searched using Trip Advisor called it and found out they had the wrong number. What will those people think of your company? Will they take the time to visit your website and try other ways to reach you?

NO! They will not because they do not have to pursue one company in 2018.

The Internet has created an "instant everything" world and has thereby nurtured a generation that will give you five to six seconds before they move on to the next thing, so you must make their time count by having the correct information in all places online.

Just like with Facebook Fan pages and social media profiles, you should optimize your profiles on directory sites with keywords that consumers will use when searching. This is vital, so any time that you can include keywords and geographic locations, use them.

- Do you have your business profiles set up so that you are everywhere that your target audience will be looking?

- Do you have enough profiles online to ensure that you do not miss prospects? The more you have the more likely you are to gain more customers when they find your information.

- Is the information on all the directory sites correct, current, and consistent? Remember that your brand will stick with consumers if you use the same colors, fonts, images, addresses, phone numbers, hours of operation, and business name.

- Are your profiles optimized to get you the best results? Keywords and geographic locations are important for all optimization.

- Do you have optimized images on your profiles?

- Do you have optimized videos on your profiles? Remember that video sells more than just pictures, so create engaging videos that showcase your knowledge and products/services.

- Do you know where your target audience likes to search? If you cannot answer "yes" to all these questions, you should contact a professional at http://mccainandassociates.com

NOTES

CHAPTER 2: WHAT WILL YOU SAY WHEN YOU FIND THEM?

Knowing what to say to your prospects and consumers is just as important as knowing where to find them.

Some would say it is more important, and I agree with them. It is wise to know what you want them to think about your brand after they encounter your ad, landing page or website.

I love sharing how business owners can get creative when communicating with their customers and their prospects. If you have detailed information about them, you can write copy that will convert. You can write ads, posts, blogs, and emails that will walk your prospects through the buying cycle and help them become paying customers.

I suggest that you spend some time creating a customer avatar. Describe your target customer. Who are they? Where do they live? How much money do they make? Are they conservative or liberal? What do they do for fun? What are their hobbies? What type charities do they support? Are they religious? When do they adopt new technology? What kind of music do they like? You get the idea. The more specific you are the better you can determine how best to engage them.

This can seem a bit daunting for most business owners and marketers alike. Knowing what to say to reach your target audience, so they can feel your sincerity and know that you do know what you are talking about can be difficult to achieve and is the reason that many advertising campaigns have poor results.

What kind of information is useful information? What does a business owner or marketing guy/girl need to write compelling copy? What questions should you ask to get you started writing copy that will attract your target audience and make the buying process easier?

My mentor, David Sprague always says, *"When value is clear, buying decisions are easier; and a confused mind will never buy."* I happen to agree with both statements because when I spoke with a prospective business owner and I could provide solutions to their challenges in a way that resonated with them, they always signed the contracts; but if I went in trying to tell them how much I knew, I often got excuses why they couldn't do business with me.

So, are you ready for some questions you should be asking to help you write better copy and close more business? Here are a few that may help you write emails, landing pages, and ad campaigns. Are you ready? I hope so. Here goes:

1. What is your unique selling proposition? What makes your business different from your competitor?
2. Describe a moment when you had an epiphany regarding your business.
3. What specific things do you want them to do?
4. What specific end results do you want to get from your product or service?
5. Why is it important for them to achieve the results?
6. Because of this I can now do _____.
7. What benefits will they get from using your product or service?
8. What are you showing them how to do?
9. Why should they listen to you?
10. What is your personal story related to this?
11. What is the pain your prospect wants to avoid?
12. How does your product/service stop the pain?
13. What were your roadblocks before you discovered your product/service?
14. What will it cost them not to have your solutions?

15. What is your product/service name?
16. How fast can they get results using your product/service?
17. What is the offer and the price?
18. What are the components of the offer?
19. Do you have an upsell? Is this a one-time offer?
20. Is there a guarantee for this offer?
21. Do you have any testimonials for this product/service?
22. What do you want them to do to take action?
23. Why should they act now?
24. What happens after they sign-up?
25. List your website address, email, phone, link to buy the offer, Facebook profile page link, and other social media profile page link

If you take your time and answer these questions before you set up a campaign, write an email, write a blog, create a website, create a landing page, or create ads, you will have better results because your message will be more concise and targeted to the right prospects.

 If you feel like this is too much to for you to do to write compelling copy and want help, go to my website http://mccainandassociates.com, and fill out the contact form. Either one of the team members or I will reach out to you quickly.

In addition to saying the right things, it is important to use technology to stay in touch with your customers and prospects. Consider creative and fun ways that you can educate your customers, your community, and prospective customers about your company.

Webinars are one of the best tools for business owners to generate new leads and to increase demand for their products and services. Webinars are also a wonderful way to educate and to use referrals to gain more customers. So why wouldn't every business owner use them?

Many of my current customers shared that they didn't know how to create a webinar or to host one. They had no idea of the tools necessary. A few even objected to the amount of time that it would take. Who has time to create and run a webinar? They were already swamped with running their businesses and just couldn't add any more to their plates.

Who cares about webinars? The answer might just surprise you. Most consumers. According to ON24, a webinar platform company, "*Webinars are the most valuable tool we have for driving leads, engaging contacts, and generating pipeline. They help us move prospects through the buying cycle, from awareness to purchase, more effectively than any other marketing tool. We use them for thought leadership, live demos, product updates, informational sessions, training, internal communications, and more. For consumers, webinars are the best way to get low information and best practices, to discover new products and services, and to see something in action before they commit to purchase.* (http://www.on24.com)" Setting up webinars can create another revenue stream for your business. The key is setting it up properly, warming your list of possible attendees effectively and engaging your list of possible participants before actual webinar date in such a way that they are eager to attend the webinar.

Selling and tracking analytics are also necessary components of a successful webinar. I guess I didn't have to include the part about selling because most business owners know that they need to make sales regularly to keep the doors open, but too many don't place enough emphasis on tracking the results.

Knowing how many people took various actions is very needed when evaluating the performance of a webinar or any campaign. With webinars, it's possible to see how many people received invitations to the webinar, how many attended, how long they viewed, and a host of other metrics that help business owners or marketers tweak the various aspects of the process to get better results. So, if you forget everything else I have said in this book up to this point, don't forget that **analytics**

matter and should be a part of everything you do to generate leads and sales. ♥

There are many webinar platforms available that will allow you to set up and run campaigns for your brand, new product/service, to educate or for any other reason. Gotomeeting.com, ON24, Google+ Hangouts, Gotowebinar, Cisco WebEx, Adobe Connect, Mega Meeting, Any Meeting, Onstream, and a host of others that will show if you do an online search.

If you decide that you want to incorporate webinars into your marketing routine, here are a few suggestions you can use to create an effective funnel:

- Generate leads or use one of your business email lists or customer lists
- Create a landing page that your prospects will go to learn about the webinar where they can opt-in/sign-up
- Create a Marketing Sequence with 2-3 emails to send to your list that will warm them up with rich content so that they are receptive and even eager to reading your next emails. The second and third emails should have the link to your

landing page with an opt-in form for them to register to attend the webinar.

- Create a voice message that you can leave for those who did not option and a separate message for those who did register. It should be short and act as a reminder.
- Set up the webinar and host it on the day you set.
- Check out your analytics to determine how to segment your list of attendees according to how long they attended and according to their buying behavior.
- Call and create an email campaign to those who did not buy from your webinar and for those who left before the webinar ended to inquire about what could have been done to keep them in attendance.
- Call those attendees who stayed on the webinar at least 50% to learn why they left, and to gauge their interest in the webinar offer. Consider a sliding offer if it will help close the sale.

- Send a list of attendees who purchased from the webinar into a Nurturing Campaign where you can continue to educate and market other products to them.
- Create an email campaign for those who did not attend the webinar and for those who left before watching 50% of the webinar to look at a Replay of the webinar with the link included.
- Repeat and tweak these steps as needed.

These steps will help you grow your business, connect with your target audience effectively, and improve your reputation because you are delivering high-quality content. Remember this is a relationship. Just like a marriage, your customers, prospects, and community will appreciate a real conversation that is full of substance rather than a shallow one about trivial things.

I encourage you to put on webinars for three months at least twice monthly and measure your results.

What is it that your customers would love to know about that you can teach them on a webinar? Which product or service would they love to know more about? What current events are occurring now that upset people but that your product/services webinar can help them be less anxious? Think outside of the box and watch how your business grows and your influence increases as you're established as a market leader.

If you are interested in learning more about setting up and running a webinar, but you do not have the time, my team and I will happily help you. Go to http://mccainandassociates.com and fill out a contact form. Include that you are interested in webinars, and we will contact you promptly. ♥

NOTES

CHAPTER 3 | DO YOU EVEN KNOW WHO THEY ARE?

The title of this chapter may seem a little silly when you first read it. Do you even know who your customers are? You're probably thinking, "*Of course I know my customers, Allison.*" But I don't mean do you know them like do they exist or not. I mean do you know the names and contact information of the customers who spend the most money with your business?

Remember, I agreed to arm you with knowledge so that you can better connect with your customers and communities. Right now, I want you to understand how important it is for your business to have a list of the people who support you by purchasing your products/services.

When I ask most business owners to name the most important aspect of their business, I get all kinds of interesting answers like the sales team, the marketing division, the advertising it does, and many others that are equally as wrong. The most important part of your business is and will always be the list of your customers! The saying "the money is in the list" is accurate. The second most important part of your business is your relationship to that list. David Sprague taught me this, and I will never forget it. You shouldn't either because if you develop a good relationship with your list, it can increase your revenues significantly.

The standard rule in marketing is that your list should provide you $1 per email you send to it per month. Yes, you read correctly. $1 per name on your list per month; so, if you have a list of your customers, and that list has 1500 people on it, you should make about $1500 from email campaigns with good offers in it.

Are you currently marketing to your list on a regular basis? If you are not, don't beat yourself up. Just determine that from today on you are going to build a list of your customers, and you are going to stay engaged with them through content-rich emails that will include at least one offer per month.

The Pareto Principle or the 80/20 Rule of Marketing: According to Vilfredo Pareto, 80% of your company's revenues come from 20% of your customers. If you apply this to the products and/or services that you offer, it means that 80% of the sales made come from 20% of the products/services. 80% of the engagements that you get on social media come from 20% of your followers. This knowledge can come in handy if you are checking your analytics on a regular basis. It can show you what types of engagements are working. What is your 20% interested in reading, viewing, answering, purchasing, sharing, liking, tweeting, retweeting, watching, and using? Knowing the answers to these questions can mean the difference between having an increase or decrease in revenue.

  Now that you have done the hard part of committing to building a list of your customers, let's look at a few ways of *how* to build it. There are many ways to do this from creating good landing pages with opt-ins, livestreaming on social media, creating quizzes and contests on social media, creating digital Sign-In forms for customers to sign when they visit your business for a service or product, creating video ads on social media with options, to permission-based Wi-Fi marketing that collects the contact information of users upon their acceptance of the terms of the agreement in exchange for letting them use your Free WI-FI, and many other ways. My favorite two are Wi-Fi Marketing and using Sign-In Forms because they have a seamlessness about them that make them very efficient. Let me tell you just a little about both.

Wi-Fi Marketing is an amazing way to build a list because whenever users log in to use the free Wi-Fi, they are required to use their login information from a social media site that has already confirmed their name and email address. In some cases, their cell phone number has also been verified, so by giving users what they want (FREE Wi-Fi), they agree to give you their contact information and permission to reach out to them at a later date with great deals and offers. Isn't it brilliant? I like to call it Win-Win because both the customer and the business owner wins. ♦♥

Once you have a list, you can reach out to them with Text Message Marketing (SMS) or emails that share future discounts, coupons, introduce new products/services, share upcoming events, and other promotions.

Wi-Fi Marketing also allows you to build another revenue stream through advertising. You can approach business owners and enable them to market to your Wi-Fi users for a monthly fee. They can present their best offers to those using your Wi-Fi. This ad revenue moves your Wi-Fi from just an additional business expense to another stream of revenue.

Sign-In Forms are like Wi-Fi Marketing in the sense that once logged in; the business owner can reach out to the customers in the future with offers, deals, coupons, discounts, and so forth. The difference is that Sign-In Forms also allow you to build your online reputation quickly! How can they do that you ask? I am glad you asked. ♦♥

When your customers come into your business, you present them with a tablet or another smart device for them to sign-in to be seen. If you have a business where you go to customers like pest control, electricians, hvac contractors, landscapers, etc., the Sign-In Form can be used as proof of service. The technician gets the customer to sign-in when they arrive at the customer's home. At that point, your employee/technician informs them that the goal is to provide 100% customer satisfaction; so, they are asking them to rate the service provided.

The beauty of the Sign-In Form is that you have the ability to direct where the reviews will go (Google, Yelp, Angie's List, Trip Advisor, etc.). If the review is at least a 4-Star review, it will be posted on the platform that the business owner requests; but if it's less than a 4-Star review, it will go to a custom-built web page that the business owner has designated so that someone from the company can quickly apologize for their displeasure and work to correct the problem.

This is HUGE because it allows your company to keep the negatives private until there has been correction. A Sign-In Form can protect you and help you build a 5-Star reputation quickly. No more being ambushed by a disgruntled customer airing their complaints online for the world to see without bothering to contact you first.

Also, now you can make sure that you are providing the top quality needed to dominate your market. The Sign-

In Form provides you with current assessments of your employees' behavior. This is important because sometimes business owners never get the chance to really see how their employees are when no one is looking. You can increase your chances of holding on to dissatisfied customers by being transparent, being willing to listen, and by making changes when appropriate. Moreover, I do not have to tell you that it is cheaper to retain a customer than to acquire a new one.

This is a general overview of Sign-In Forms that my company offers. There may be other businesses that do similar things, but none will care about you achieving your desired results as much as my team and I do. If you do not have a Sign-In Form and you want to improve your online reputation, contact us. My team is always available to you. Fill out a contact form at http://mccainandassociates.com, and someone will reach out to you promptly.

NOTES

CHAPTER 4 | WHAT DO THEY WANT, AND WHAT DO THEY THINK?

No one will ever convince me that knowing what people want isn't critical to business success. I am not talking about what you think they want either. I mean what do your customers want from you? What kind of product/service could you offer them that they would not only buy right on the spot, but they would tell their family and friends about also? What is your business doing that turns your customers off? Are your employees as nice to your clients when you are not there? Are your restrooms clean? Was the food cold when it arrived? Did your customers have to wait an incredible length of time before being served? Did the receptionist who answered the phone get rude with a caller? Was your customer put on hold for longer than 15-30 seconds?

These are the types of questions that you need to know the answers to if you hope to have a profitable business long-term. So, how do you go about getting these answers? You could foolishly think that if a customer has not complained to you that everything must be all right, but you would be doing your business an injustice because many people may not want to confront you in person, but they will leave a review about your company online in the privacy of their home. If some of your customers don't feel comfortable enough to tell you about their issues with your company, how can you find out what's really going on? How will you know if your business is as great as you think it is?

Create a series of Feedback Pages that ask the questions you really need to have answered to make informed decisions about your company's customer service. Feedback pages can include a welcome video from you with the following types of survey questions:

- about products/services,

- about employees,

- about the physical condition of the business,

- about the overall customer service experience.

You determine the social media platforms where you want the positive reviews to go, and you determine what you want on the page for the negative reviews. This includes a video apologizing for the bad experience, questions about different parts of your business along with a place for them to discuss their issues. You can also include some of your 5-Star reviews from other satisfied customers to show that your business and employees normally function at the highest levels of excellence and that their negative experience is out of the norm. This is one of the most effective and creative ways to always know how things are going at your business. Here is a sample Feedback Page that a client in the Transportation industry used with his taxi customers.

This Feedback Page has two pages, and the one on the previous page is the first page. You can include testimonials, videos, and images if you like. The most important thing to remember is to ask the questions that you need to know. I have found if you create an opportunity for your customers to help you make your business better, many will participate.

You should get to know your customers to know how much communication with them is too much, how much is not enough, and how much is just right. There are many theories out there, but none of them can take the place of you knowing your customers. They will let you know what works and what doesn't; so, don't miss out on this incredible resource you have. Creating Feedback Pages can be just the thing you need to take your business to the next level, so get busy creating yours.

If you need help creating Feedback Pages, fill out a contact form or opt-in for a FREE consultation on my website http://mccainandassociates.com. We will be happy to help you get your page created ASAP. ♦♥

NOTES

CHAPTER 5 | YOU GOTTA KEEP THEM INTERESTED

By now you are probably thinking, "*Allison, I know I need to keep them interested, but for the life of me I do not know how to do that.*" If that is you, don't worry because I have got you covered. Once you use your feedback pages for a few months, you will get a sense of who your customers are and the things they like. As you learn more about them, you will engage with them on social media sites, and you will keep them informed about things going on with your business. I usually hate clichés, but "*your customers do not care how much you know until they know how much you care*" is true; so, let them know you care various in email campaigns.

Think again of the relationship between and man and his wife. Until he or she knows that the other person is vested in the relationship for the long term, there are certain intimacies that may never happen. For example, that woman may never have an intimate relationship with you if she perceives you to be dating many people at the same time as her. But once she knows that she is your one and only, she will give you just about anything you want. Your customers operate kind of the same way. The love knowing what's going on with your business because they are vested in you. They are loyal to you and love your products/services; so, they want to be kept in the loop. Here are a few things you can and should email them about:

- Tell them when you've got new products and services;

- let them know when prices change;

- inform them when something on the news that affects your industry pisses you off;

- share when a community event is worth supporting;

- let them know when your spouse is expecting a baby and give them a discount coupon;

- ask their opinions;

- let them know you're thinking about them on the holidays;

- tell them Happy Birthday;

- tell them Happy Anniversary;

- tell them Merry Christmas or its equivalent;

- tell them Happy New Year;
- share all the main holidays with them by offering them personal pictures and a special promotion.

Do you get the idea? Your customers will feel as important as you make them feel by the way you interact with them. So, don't shy away from using email to stay connected to your customers and your social media community.

There are many email autoresponders that will help you create the campaigns your business needs to automate your communication process. Mail Chimp, AWeber, Get Response, Constant Contact, and many others are available.

You can segment those on your lists who buy from those who do not. You can even segment those who opened your email vs. those who did not. Segment those who opened and email and clicked on a link vs those who did not. Autoresponders will help you assess which emails are getting results and which are not.

You can test subject lines, the text of the emails, the images used in the emails and other things to determine what is working and what is not working. It is critical that you do split testing consistently and make corrections until you find the perfect recipe for sending emails that get you results. This is a tool that is vitally necessary if you want to get to the place of earning $1 per email each month. After all, that is the goal. ♦♥

NOTES

CHAPTER 6 | GIVE THEM WHAT THEY WANT

Now, Allison, you do not know my customers or me, so how can you tell me what they want? That is a good question, and the answer is even better. You give them what ALL consumers want: **deals**! That is right, give your customers a great deal weekly, bi-weekly, or monthly, and they will get you new customers.

One of the greatest ways that you can do this is by creating Deals Sites like Groupon or Living Social. This is one of the greatest tools that a business owner has at his/her disposal to create fast cash flow because people love getting good things with big discounts. They will often buy more of the things because they are cheaper. They will often share their huge savings across most social media platforms with their family and friends.

Groupon and Living Social are great deals sites, but they take so much of the profits from business owners, that the deals end up costing the business owner money rather than making them money. **You do not need to give up 50-70% of your profits to have a great deal page and to sell lots of your products/services.** You can set up a great offer and still make a profit.

This needs to be a product/service that is discounted enough to be a deal. I like the 35-45% revshare with business owners when I create Deals Sites. This means that I will create the sites, set up the deals, create the ads that generate traffic to the sites and the business owner will get 65% of every sale made; I will make 35% of every sale.

Keep in mind that for this to work, the Deal must be something that your customers, your social media community, and your prospects will want, so don't just put your discontinued items or things you want to get rid of here. Give them one of your best sellers at a discounted rate. Then put a timer on how long they have to buy it. Include a social media icon that they can use to share their deals. Include some of the features and benefits of this product/service; and add a short video of the items in use and you are on your way to having a great campaign. The last thing you need to do is send some traffic to your deals page. You can use your lists if they have enough people on them. I advise creating ads on Facebook, Twitter, YouTube, Google, or other social media sites depending on the deal because you can customize your audience and get the best results. You would be amazed at the kinds of numbers you can get from a modest budget of $30-$40/day.

Here is a sample of a deal page that I used to sell videos

to businesses.

Both images make up this Deals Site.

Click here to see the video for the Deal:
https://youtu.be/wq64REn8Nfw

If you send the right traffic to the right deal, you are going to create a tsunami of sales! The seasons changing, holidays, birthdays, and anniversaries are wonderful reasons to offer deals, so get started now. Setting up and running a Deals Campaign can result in an increase of warm prospects in your lists as well as in new customers and more cash flow. Don't let the first day of Spring, St. Patrick's Day, Presidents' Day, Memorial Day, 4th of July, Black Friday, Small Business Saturday, Cyber Monday, Christmas, and New Year's sales pass you by. Create your Deals Page and make all four quarters of this year your best yet!

If you need help in creating a Deals Page, building a list, and marketing to them in email and text message campaigns later fill out a contact form on my website http://mccainandassociates.com, and someone will contact you as soon as possible.

NOTES

CHAPTER 7 | DO YOU KNOW WHAT OTHERS ARE SAYING ABOUT YOU?

This is one of the most important questions that you must answer to help your business grow and to establish yourself as a market leader. Knowing what people think about your business helps you to make corrections when and where needed. Knowing what people are saying about you also lets you know to do more of the things that work to increase sales, cashflow, and revenue. So how else can you find out what your customers think about you without using Feedback Pages?

If you guessed getting a FREE copy of your business' Online Reputation Report (ORP), you guessed right!

Your ORP is one of the greatest tools available for any business because in it is the proof of what your customers really think about your business. Just like your credit report is proof of how you pay your bills, your ORP is proof of how your customers perceive your business. It covers all aspects of your business that a customer is a part of and can rate.

Your Online Reputation Report also grades your business on if it is on the most popular directory sites, social media sites, and if the content is the same across all of them. It also grades your visibility on video sites like YouTube and Vimeo because those sites have hundreds of million people viewing them daily.

If this were not enough by itself for you to receive great value, your Online Reputation Report also contains your customers' reviews of your business left on review sites like Google, Yelp, Facebook, etc. the last six months. This part alone is powerful because you get to see the good, the bad, and the ugly and fix what needs fixing.

"Allison, what should you be included in a reputation report?" This is a great question because many companies sell reputation management, but not all of them are as comprehensive as my firm's reputation report. So, let's dive in and examine our reputation report more closely than the overview I just gave you.

The four scores that are used to score a business in my reputation report are 1) **Your visibility score**, 2) **Your reputation grade**, 3) **Your video visibility grade**, and 4) **Negative reviews posted within the last six months.** Each of these parts needs to be as high as possible because this helps position your firm in the marketplace and solidifies you as an authority figure.

Visibility:

As I mentioned earlier, being found in the places where you customers and prospects are looking is vitally important to you getting more customers and increasing your revenue. The first score in your reputation report will reveal if your business is in most major business directories and if the information that is listed is the same across all sites.

The report will also offer specific solutions to the problems found that my team can execute for you.

Reputation Grade:

Your reputation grade will share the major directories that have your customer reviews listed and the directories on which your company needs to have reviews listed. Not having any reviews is as bad as having bad reviews in the same way that having no credit is perceived as negative as having bad credit. The report shows what you need and your average star rating.

Video Visibility:

This score tells whether you have videos on search engines, on the home page of your website and video sharing sites. This is important because 90% of consumers watched videos last week, and 70% say that videos help them to make buying decisions.

Negative Reviews:

The Reputation Report will also list any negative reviews posted about your company. It will show how many have been posted in the last six months, so we can develop tactics and strategies to push the negative reviews down by posting more good reviews. Remember, the Sign-In Form will facilitate this process.

For those businesses that have a 5-Star reputation, the next step is to market it to generate new customers. Showcasing the reviews in video format or in creative images on social media sites will allow your customers to share them with their family and friends. Increase your visibility and build a great reputation, so you can help more customers.

My firm will help you to build, manage, and market your great reputation in many ways. If you want to know what your customers have been saying about you and know if your business profiles are congruent and on the major directory and review sites and know whether you have a strong enough video visibility you should contact me to get your FREE Reputation Report. It normally costs $149, and you're getting it absolutely FREE just because you purchased my book. ♦♥

Fill out a contact form on my website http://mccainandassociates.com, and include that you want your FREE report, and either a team member or I will contact you promptly.

NOTES

CHAPTER 8 | JUST SAY PLEASE

Sometimes we make our lives more complicated when it does not have to be. I remember as a little girl, I would ask my mom for chips or a popsicle, and she normally would ask me this question: "What's the magic word?" I would immediately answer, "Please"; and she would reward me with my request. This was the way I grew up, and it has made such a lasting impression in my life that I often use it in my business.

When I meet with clients who have a lower reputation score than they want, one of my first questions is "What have you done to improve your score?" More times than not, the answer is they do not know what to do. Thinking back to things that have worked well for me, I often suggest that they simply ask their customers to leave them a review and always to say please. You may be thinking that sounds too simple, but it works

You can use the Sign-In Form to ask for reviews from your current customers, or you can create an email sequence where you ask for reviews and say please. Email marketing is a very effective way to cultivate and nurture your relationships with your customers, so sharing your goal of creating a culture of excellence in your business may work towards getting your customers to pitch in and help.

As with the other email campaigns, you need to use a list of your customers who have visited your business recently. Teach them about why your reputation is important. Share what you stand for and what they should expect from you and your staff as it relates to customer service and high-quality services. I suggest including a video of yourself sharing from your heart. You can include an image of yourself with a play button and include the link to the video, so when they click on the play button, they're taken to the actual video. The video should be one minute to a minute and a half in duration because anything longer will lose your customers.

I cannot discuss this email campaign without warning you about a danger associated with getting online reviews. **It is illegal to pay or incentivize customers into leaving good reviews.** The Federal Trade Commission (FTC) will file charges against you if you're caught doing this. Reviews must be sincere and based on doing business with a business. What does incentivizing customers look like? You cannot give your customers a discount in exchange for them leaving you a review. The reason for this is that Google, Amazon, and other big companies want their customers to have the best experience while using their platform.

So, if they purchase an item or do business with a company that has a 5-Star review rating based on payments-for-reviews, the customer's experience may not be the same as in the fake reviews, and that will not work. If you want a 5-Star reputation, then you must do the work to get there. It's okay if you have a low reputation score now because we can help you fix it; but it will likely include developing a business culture of excellence. This means all parts of the company must be on the same page. There should be proper training about what excellence looks like in each department of the company. Take the time to invest in your business' reputation, and you will reap a harvest of loyal and repeat customers sending you referrals consistently.

So, if you want to thank your customers for taking time out of their day to share a review, think about it. The penalties for violating this policy can include being banned from using the various platforms. This can create a financial burden on your business that you don't need. To avoid this, don't offer any incentives in exchange for leaving reviews.

NOTES

CHAPTER 9 | WHO DID WHAT? WHEN? WHY?

If someone walked into your business right now and offered to pay you $1,000 if you could produce data that included the last 5 customer transactions with his or her birthdates, their total spending year-to-date with your business, and the length of time they have been your customers, would you be able to collect the $1,000?

Some industries depend on this level of attention to detail in their daily activities, but most do not. This attention to detail will take your business to the next level; and if you do not have a way to organize your marketing and sales activities based on the actual numbers related to your business, then again, you are leaving money on the table.

Now that you recognize that you have been leaving money on the table by not being organized and having an automated system to keep up with the business activity in your firm, what do you do now? How do you fix it? There are many solutions, but the one that I think can make the biggest impact in your business is the CRM tool.

Getting Customer Relationship Management (CRM)

software will help you learn more about your business than you can imagine. Your CRM is a system for managing client interactions, dealing with future and current customers, optimizing and systematizing relationships.

The CRM is the part of your business that shows that you aren't just looking for a casual relationship with your customers. It is the tool that keeps track of the important data about them. Remember the married couple example I used earlier in the book. The CRM is like getting proposed to by your significant other. It says that you are committed to them for the long-haul and you want to be with them in good and bad times. The CRM kind of does the same thing for your customers—taking them from being paying customers to being loyal customers.

Developing relationships with your customers is one of the smartest investments a business owner can do to insure their longevity. This means you must have a way to gather information about your customers and prospects, a way to follow up with them, a way to provide relevant, interesting content to them, and of course a way to give them great deals and promotions.

Because there are so many companies still treating their customers like simple transactions, the marketplace is ripe for business owners to lead with relationships, and a CRM tool is the first step in revving up your connections with your customers.

When you first get started with your CRM, you may be a bit overwhelmed because the good ones are quite comprehensive. Don't let this deter you from learning to use them effectively because once you do; you will wonder how you ever got along without them. They are designed to collect and organize useful data that can help you ultimately satisfy your customers' needs through products and services your company provides.

CRM tools will let you import a list of your customers and keep detailed records of each one. Purchases, preferences, transaction details, personal information like birthdates, anniversaries, number of children, and other relevant data is stored in each file. The more you know about your customers, the better you will be able to serve them, and this kind of service will yield high profits and a 5-Star reputation.

The CRM will have a history of who did what when where why and how that can be helpful if any problems come up later. Take it from me, when you have a customer call with a complaint, and your employee can open the CRM and repeat what happened with them, when they came into your business last, and other information specific to them, it will send the message that they are important to your business. That is the message you want all your customers to receive.

Your CRM tool will also allow any employee to work with your customers to handle and solve challenges efficiently because it includes notes from every action taken with the customer. I'm sure I don't have to tell you how good it feels when you call up your favorite home improvement store like Lowes to get some more of the flowers that you ordered last year, and the representative who answers gets some information from you and can pull your file and tell you the exact name of those flowers. They can do that because they have a CRM tool, and it ROCKS!

In addition to all the customer data, CRM tools also provide a snapshot of the sales pipeline from gathering leads to closing the deal to when the next follow-up is to be scheduled; so, you know where you are production wise at all times. Good CRMs will allow you to import sales scripts, have calling features to dial leads, have a notes section for each call; comes with a section to integrate autoresponders for emails, have a section for the amounts of each deal pending, allows you to include an inventory of all products and services with pricing, calendars to set appointments, and an area covering various stages of the sales cycle, and everything else that your employees need to sell more intentionally.

Again, most CRM tools will have features that will allow you to automate your business processes and systems that include product deployment, contact management, customer support, email marketing, interaction tracking, lead management, and marketing automation. You can accurately track all business opportunities and close more deals in less time.

You can also identify bottlenecks in the sales processes from your sales pipeline at a view, well in advance and effectively utilize existing customer data from event analytics for future cross-selling and upselling opportunities.

The right CRM tool will provide you with the analytics you need to evaluate what is working and what is not. This is paramount when running various campaigns because as David Sprague says, *"The numbers tell you what to do; and your future success depends on your daily tasks."* I'll take it a step further and add, your daily tasks should be a part of your CRM and provide you with the actions you need to take to achieve your daily, weekly, monthly, quarterly, and annual goals.

If you do not have a CRM tool, and see the value in having one and learning to use it, go to my website http://mccainandassociates.com and fill out a contact form. Either a team member or I will contact you

ASAP.

Don't wait to get your CRM and begin developing better customer relationships now. This could be the difference between success and failure in your business. Plan to spend 2018 focused on your customers, and you will be surprised at your results.

NOTES

CHAPTER 10 | ALWAYS SAY THANK YOU

Saying *Thank You* seems like a simple thing to do because we're raised hearing that, but I want to remind you that the timeless quality of good manners is a better strategy for connecting with people than most people think. Whether you say, "Thank You, Thanks, Gracias, Merci, Grazie, Arigato, or Danke Sehr" very few people will not appreciate hearing these words. I have thought about how hearing these words makes me feel as a person, and I have got to admit that it makes me smile.

When I do something for my children, and they say thank you, I immediately tell them that they are welcome; and it makes me feel appreciated. The same is true when my customers tell me that. It makes me feel good to think I have pleased them, and I want to share it. So, in the spirit of Thanksgiving, I set up a campaign to let my customers know that I appreciated them very much. I call this my Thank You Campaign. Initially, I emailed 89 clients and told them that I was thankful for their business, and to show that I appreciated them, I sent them a coupon for a FREE, ($1500-value) Testimonial video that they could use to market a 5-Star review that one of their customers left for them. My customers are business owners who have customers of their own, so they very quickly saw the value in the video. I started the *Thank You* Campaign and was surprised at the responses I got. 34 of my clients called me to ask if the email was a hoax. I assured them that it was not. They wanted to know why I did this, so I shared the epiphany I had regarding the power of giving thanks.

What was the result? I have clients who are more loyal to me and who trust me. Is it worth it to you to bless someone's life? How would it make you feel to know that you did something that could help a fellow business owner look good online? I challenge you to give thanks in a small way to your family, your friends, your employees, your grocer, your cashier, your co-workers and the many other people who bless your lives in any way for the next 30 days. I promise you that what you will get in return will outweigh anything you've given.

For those of you who want to create your own *Thank You* Campaign, it is easy to do. Create your email with your giveaway included. I happen to think that adding a 30-60 seconds video is more personable and will resonate with your customers more. Your customers get to hear your tone, see your face, and do all the things we do when determining if someone is sincere or just hustling. ☺ Load your list into your autoresponder or CRM. Make sure that your email list is current to ensure that you do not get into hot water with your email company. I encourage you to create an opt-in on a landing page, so you can segment your list into those who clicked on the link to receive the gift and those who did not. Adding a retargeting pixel to your emails will allow you to track the responses and follow-up with those who didn't click to get the gift.

Also, you can get software that will notify you when your emails are opened. This tool alone is worth its weight in salt because it allows you to contact them soon after they open your email. Your success rates will skyrocket. I promise. Remember the relationship tips I've been using to parallel the level of relationships needed to connect and engage with your customers? Well, here is another one. When your significant other comes home from work and gives you a gift out of the blue with a note that says, "*I am so thankful to have you in my life because you make it so much better. Thank you for loving me and for being my wife/husband.*" How does that make you feel? That is the way you want your customers, your social media communities, and your prospective customers to feel when they get your Thank You email and gift. It will endear them to your business. I promise.

If you do not have the time in your already busy schedule to create a Thank You Campaign, visit my website http://mccainandassociates.com and fill out a contact form. A team member or I will contact you promptly.

NOTES

CHAPTER 11 | CREATE A CULTURE OF EXCELLENCE

This is by far one of the most important things that you can ever do for your business because it will linger on long after you are gone. It's so important that I'm going to mention it again. What others say about you is your reputation, and if enough people say the same things, it becomes the legacy you leave in the world.

When you work smart, treat people good, over-deliver value, and do what you say you're going to do, you create a reputation for Excellence. People will tell others, and after a while, your business will become synonymous with distinction, superiority, and top-quality. Don't believe me? I know you believe me because you are doing business in the 21st century, where word-of-mouth can make your business or kill it.

One of the things I think helps a business build and maintain a 5-Star reputation is teaching and training your staff to cultivate a spirit of excellence. This requires that you intentionally create a system where you train your employees and staff on the importance of customer service and how to handle disgruntled customers.

My company often creates customized instructional systems for business owners. We produce 5-10 videos that explain various subjects regarding online reputation and how it affects everything from your advertising costs to your location on search engines. Each person will get their own custom login and password.

Each video has a short quiz that your employees/staff must pass with a score of at least 80. After each quiz is taken, it is quickly graded. Both you and the employees/staff are emailed the grade. If the grade does not meet the threshold requirement, they must re-take it. This ensures that everyone is on the same playing field with regards to 5-Star Reputation best practices.

This training system affords you the right to create a workplace where your customers are prioritized and valued. When something happens to upset them, your employees/staff will know how to handle the situation because they have been taught it. They will know the warning signs of a situation escalating and will be able to act accordingly. This often makes the difference in whether a customer blasts your business online or comes back to shop with again.

We can include other topics for training that you want if you tell us. In addition to the Learning Center that we can create for your business, we also can create and launch webinars to train employees as well as customers. These types of activities keep you engaged, not just with your customers, but also with your employees/staff. It is important for them to have a way to voice any discrepancies without fear of retaliation. The Feedback Pages work well for employees to voice their opinions in a safe way without fear of retaliation. Once they are assured that they work in a safe place free from that, many will work harder and be more productive.

Excellence is not something businesses are born achieving. It takes consistent actions, day-in-and-day-out to inspire people to perform to your expectations.

If you want to see what companies who invest a lot to be the best places to work and that have been voted the best customer-centered businesses, do a search online. I did, and Glassdoor listed these top 10 companies as follows:

1. **Airbnb**: They have amazing people, vibrant workplace and unbeatable culture, great leadership, a diverse workforce, meals made in-house, beautiful office space, frequent happy hours, and handmade energy bars.

2. **Bain and Company**: They provide a supportive culture, competitive pay, an unparalleled colleague pool, high-impact clients.
3. **Guidewire**: They offer continuous opportunities to grow, good compensation, small company vibe, and a diverse environment
4. **Hubspot**: They focus on employee growth across all divisions, have tuition reimbursement, stocked kitchen, and motivated coworkers.
5. **Facebook**: They have chef-prepared meals, a generous parental leave policy, and caring managers.
6. **LinkedIn**: They have great perks, inspiring leadership, competitive compensation, and incredible work-life balance
7. **Boston Consulting Group**: They have "smart colleagues, great teams, excellent culture.
8. **Google**: They offer food, gyms, discounts, great people working there
9. **Nestle Purina PetCare**: They are "people-oriented" and value work-life-balance; they allow pets at work.

10. **Zillow**: They offer free foods, snacks, and amazing views; and they have a transparent executive team.

(http://www.entrepreneur.com/slideshow/253741)

According to Entrepreneur.com, "to be on this list, companies had to employ more than 1,000 people and have received at least 50 approved company Glassdoor reviews in the past year. The overall ranking was determined based on the quantity, quality, and consistency of these reviews." Do you notice how many times they speak about working with good people? This caught my eye as well as the number that included something about the culture of the business.

Don't just assume that your employees/staff know how to treat your customers. Train them up in the way they should behave, and you can trust that your reputation will reflect it.

NOTES

CHAPTER 12 | LET THEM KNOW HOW GREAT YOU ARE

I once heard the sales phenom, Grant Cardone, say something that I never forgot. He stated that *"the number one threat to your business being exceedingly successful is your obscurity…no one knows that you exist and that you can help them."* I pondered that statement for months. Eventually my mind accepted that this was a true statement. It resonated in my spirit, and I knew it to be true of me. Where would my company be if more people knew that I existed and that I could help them grow their business and I could help them get to the next level?

If more of the right people knew what products and services you offered and knew the quality of work and the spirit of excellence that governs your business, more of them would do business with you, and your life would be changed forever.

Once upon a time, being well-known was hard to achieve, and only those who were wealthy enough to advertise on tv and other means could afford it. With the emergence and growth of the Internet, social media, video sharing sites, live streaming capabilities, and mobile devices, the world is flatter. Barriers to starting and growing a business are few and within an arm's reach. Don't believe me? Well, see if you can answer a few of the following questions for me:

1. How did Justin Bieber come to Usher Raymond's attention?
2. How did Journey find their now lead singer, Arnel Pineda?
3. How did model, Kate Upton grow her modeling business to become an international model?
4. What platform helped Soulja Boy get his start and earn more than $7 million in his first year.
5. How did Mark Zuckerberg become a billionaire?
6. How did Havard Rugland get from playing Rugby to being on the Detroit Lion's NFL team?
7. How did singer-song writer, Shawn Mendes get the attention of record executives?
8. How did Yuya create an income stream of $41,000/month?

9. How did Jenna Marbles amass a net worth of around $2.5 million dollars doing what she loves?

If you guessed some social media or video streaming site, you are correct. The first three and Havard Rugland in the list got their start on YouTube; Soulja Boy started on MySpace. Zuckerberg is the genius behind Facebook. Jenna Marbles creates funny videos on YouTube; and Shawn Mendes got his start on the The Vine app. They each went from obscurity by routinely posting and sharing videos and growing a following. This is part of the American Dream.

Now, what does this have to do with you? I am glad you asked. If you start a few social media profiles and video sharing profiles, you can increase your visibility. The people I listed above invested in themselves and were disciplined to work on this daily regardless of how they felt, and it paid off in spades. You can too.

One of the things that I encourage you to do is to create a series of videos in which your followers on subject matters related to your business. If you don't feel comfortable doing this, pay an employee to build you a community of followers by sharing valuable information. Provide entertaining content daily. Some of this you will want to share yourself since it will help to solidify you as a subject matter expert. My team often creates Expert Videos for my customers that work in this space.

Here is a sample Expert Video we created for a customer. Click the video below to play it.

Answer questions on blogs, groups, and forums, and reply to others' posts. Before you know it, people will follow you and share your broadcasts and videos with others.

Post images of your 5-Star reviews on as many social media sites and ask your friends to share them. You can also post Testimonial and Expert videos on those same sites.

If you do not currently live stream, start! This has got to be one of the fastest ways to build a following and to gain influence. Periscope, Facebook Live, Instagram, Snap Chat, Google+ Hangouts, and other platforms will allow you to engage with your customers in a more personal way. Sharing your expertise this way gives you an opportunity to get direct feedback on what your customers want and don't want from your brand.

If you need Expert Videos, Testimonials, Social Media posting, and any other strategy found in this book, check out my website http://mccainandassociates.com and fill out a contact form. Either a team member or I will reach out to you as soon as possible. I look forward to speaking with you.

Remove all limitations and strengthen your connections with your customers. You really can grow the business of your dreams, make a great living, build and leave a legacy of excellence with a 5-Star reputation.

NOTES

CHAPTER 13 | ARE YOU REACHING THE RIGHT PEOPLE?

I struggled with if I should include this chapter since I spoke about it throughout other chapters, and after much deliberation, I decided this is worth mentioning in its own chapter because it's very important. Who is your target audience? Does your business service individuals or businesses? Do you have a way to constantly generate new leads? This is one of the most important parts of your business, so it should be prioritized and automated.

What does automating do for your reputation? I'm glad you asked. Automating your lead generation process allows you to continuously add new prospects into your sales pipeline on purpose. If your target audience is consumers, then advertising on social media sites may be the best way to connect with the right people. However, if your target audience is other business owners, you need a way to reach those leads. With the right tools, you can find the businesses that need your products/services and make sure they know that you can help them.

Adding leads into your email campaigns is a way to

share your company's mission and values while offering valuable offers. Targeting your leads will weed out the customers who are not a good fit for you. Once you find the right companies, it is important that you identify the problems that you can solve for them and create a personalized plan customized just for them.

Don't waste your emails with salesy language that only turns off your prospect. Lead with value. Ask the right questions. Listen for where they are experiencing pain, and over-deliver value. Offer a discounted price or free trial period. Be flexible. Focus on helping your leads grow their business, and as a result, you will grow yours.

Generating leads is to your business what gas is to your automobile. My company provides lead generation services for B2B firms. We have fresh, targeted leads that need at least one common marketing service. For example, if you sell website design our tools will find the businesses in a specific city and state that do not have websites, so you can reach out to them. Our technology is state of the art and innovative. Some of the things it will find out about a business are:

- Owner's Name
- Business Address
- Business Email and Phone
- Website

- Google Ranking
- Is there video on first page of website?
- Citations
- Google Score
- Google Reviews
- Google Reviewer's Name
- Does the business have a deal on Groupon or Living Social offer?
- Does the company have a mobile optimized website?
- Is the website a mobile responsive site?
- Company's current PPC Daily Spend
- Company's current PPC Monthly Spend
- Website Backlinks
- Search Volume
- Keywords
- Google Analytics
- Phone in text format
- Facebook, Twitter, Google+, YouTube connections
- Google+ Url

- Facebook Url, Likes, Shares, People Talking About, and Social Score
- Twitter Url, Number of Tweets, and Followers

We provide this information and more to help you reach the business owners who need your services. Don't let your business plateau. Breathe life into it with consistent and qualified leads.

If you're interested in getting targeted B2B leads, visit my website at http://mccainandassociates.com and fill out the contact form. Include LEADS on your form.

NOTES

CHAPTER 14 | FUNNEL MAGIC

Another thing that you can do to connect with your audience and automate your sales process is to create funnels. Creating funnels is one of the few things that you can do for your business that, if done correctly, will produce immediate results. What exactly is a funnel? Let me answer that by giving you an example of one of the best funnel systems on the planet. Do you remember going to McDonald's and ordering a hamburger and the person taking your order asked you, *"Would you like fries with that and a drink?"* This is an example of a funnel. Offering additional items that complement your original offer, so that you make more money.

Funnels are an amazing way for you to upsell additional products/services to increase the amount that you're able to make from each customer. The challenge is that most businesses only sell individual products thereby limiting their ability to create an effective funnel.

I bet you've heard the cliché *make money while you sleep*. The people who can do so have created funnels that automate the buying process with multiple items. They have created a system that will lead their customers from one product they love to another that will enhance the one just purchased and is followed by another that will be the icing on the cake; then to make sure that they have everything they need with the products, they may offer a one-on-one consultation or a mastermind invitation for a higher cost. Before long, the customer has purchased three items instead of just one. This is an overly simplified funnel, but you get the gist of what I'm saying.

Creating a sales funnel is the best way to utilize your leads and increase your margins so you can make two to three times as much for each sale. You create a sales process that may include two- four products or more. Now think about emailing great deals to your 20% customers who are giving you 80% of your revenue. What would it do to your bottom line if you could get these loyal customers to spend three times as much each month? This could be a game changer for you.

I learned about funnels from one of the smartest businessmen I know: Russel Brunson. He not only shared about the importance of a business owner creating funnels to achieve business success; but he created a system with many different funnels and other tools that will help companies earn more with the advertising they are currently using. You may have heard of Click Funnels. It's one of Russell's signature products and is used by millions of business owners around the world. Google him to get your free trial.

He has helped me grow my business, so I know the importance of funnels in growing *your* business and keeping you connected with your customers and prospects on a deeper level.

Creating and executing the right funnels require you to narrow down who your target customer is and to know where they buy their _____. Once you know who they are and where they buy, you are well on your way to figuring out what you can use to attract them to your company and get them to purchase your products/services. Which funnel will work best for each campaign you run?

This can be a challenging process if you're doing it alone, but it doesn't have to be. Our firm has dedicated funnel specialists waiting to help you build the right funnel for your business. You can learn how to make more from each sale so that you're able to sell more. Visit http://mccainandassociates.com and fill out a contact form. Someone will reach out to you quickly.

NOTES

SUMMARY

I hope you found this book to contain at least one thing with which you can take immediate action. Building a 5-Star reputation will be the result of how you and your employees/staff engage and interact with your customers. It's never too late to get started! Today can completely change how your story will end. Focus on leading with value every day. Know your numbers so that you can make business decisions based on data and not just emotion.

Remember the things your mom taught you when you were a child: Say Please and Thank You. Share your knowledge in the right places with the right people. Do not be afraid to ask your customers what they like and don't like about your business and use that information to customize your products/sales. And finally, do not forget to invest in your business. Hire a professional who can help you take your business to the next level. What are you waiting for to start building the life and business you want? Now is the time, so get started.

ABOUT THE AUTHOR

Allison McIntyre Cain is a wife, a mother, a mother-in-law, a grandmother, a sister, and a daughter. She loves helping business owners grow their businesses by using technology effectively, and she believes that local businesses are the cornerstone of most communities. She grew up in a rural community and has a love for education. This doesn't have to be a formal education like college because that is not the way for everyone.

Learning new things is the best thing that anyone wanting to better themselves can do. It is a way out of so many challenging situations. Allison has a BS in Logistics Management and an MBA with a concentration in Marketing. She has a passion for helping individuals dream again and make those dreams a reality through hard work and resilience.

www.ingramcontent.com/pod-product-compliance
Lightning Source LLC
Chambersburg PA
CBHW060352190526
45169CB00002B/572